Gem(GS)Star™

PRESENTS

TO: Mollie

Thank you so much for facilitating the bereavement & art therapy activities to help us in the healing process. It is so greatly appreciated.

God's blessings Always!

Much Love,
Miss Brit
(Brittany)

Real Talk

Quotes to Get You Through to Becoming a Better YOU!

by

Miss Brit

Published by
Gem Star™
P.O. Box 20157
Cleveland, Ohio 44120

Real Talk: Quotes to Get You Through to Becoming a Better YOU!
Copyright © 2011 by Miss Brit

Disclaimer: All quotes and comments are originally written by Miss Brit. Anything similar is coincidental.

All rights reserved, including the right of reproduction in whole or in part in any form. No part of this book may be used or reproduced in any manner, whatsoever, without permission except in the case of brief quotations embodied in critical articles and reviews. For information, address Gem Star™, P.O. Box 20157, Cleveland, OH 44120 or email gemstarmedia1@yahoo.com.

All Gem Star™ books may be purchased for education, business, or sales promotional use. For information, please write to Gem Star™, P.O. Box 20157, Cleveland, OH 44120

ISBN: 978-0-9836582-0-7

Library of Congress Control Number: 2011935443

Category: Inspirational/Young Adult/Non-Fiction/Self Help

All theme creations/drawings by Luciana Luraschi
All concepts by Miss Brit
All quotes are original works by Miss Brit
Book Designer: Luciana Luraschi
Interior Layout: TWA Solutions

My Thanks...

All credit to God for the opportunity to publish this book. Thank You God for all that You are. Thank You Jesus for being my Lord and Savior. I love You always!

To my wonderful mom, dad and Grammy Mary who always encouraged my creative writing/drawing very early on. Love you all! I appreciate your inspiration!

P. S. Thank you mom for always believing in me! Thank you dad for keeping my vocabulary on point! Thank you Grammy Mary for drawing with me and showing me your artistic creativity throughout my childhood.

Thank you to my Grandma Ora: you were a great listener and spoke great words of wisdom and truth...Rest in Heaven.

Thank you to **all** my additional family, friends and supporters distant and near. I love you all the same! Thank you to each and every person who has ever shown me kindness. Thank you to everyone who has been there for me. My gratitude and love to all of you.

Thank you so much Luciana for all the amazing work on this book project and my company brand. Thank you for your patience through every aspect of this project. Your creativity is astounding!

To Eryka, thank you for your time, feedback and expertise on my first book project. Special thanks to Theresa for your advice and concern. Thank you for keeping it real with me about the challenges of the self publishing business. You are a true professional!

Thank you to Jessica at TWA Solutions for your patience, honesty and kindness. Sorry if I forgot anyone! To everyone who reads this book: Let us all be an encouragement to one another. Be a light in the world and let the goodness in you shine through! God's love and blessings to everyone always!!!!

Love,
Miss Brit

Love God

Appreciate Life

Love You

And Only Then You Can Truly Love Others!

This book is dedicated to everyone because we all need encouragement and truth.

As I heard someone say in a local coffee shop, life is too beautiful to be miserable.

⇛ ⇛ ⇛ ⇛ ⇛

Real Intro...

Since I was very young, I've always enjoyed the creativity that writing offers. Over the years, I've been able to practice and grow in my writing because of the advancement of modern technology. Blogging daily and inspirational thoughts have inspired me to write this book. After all, each and every one of us could use words to cheer us up or to give us food for thought. It is very easy to get distracted with the daily happenings of life. In saying that, this book is full of thoughts to be a part of setting the tone for your entire day.

We often allow the pressures of society and the media (in which is us, the people) dictate our lives and stress us out. In many cases, we try to constantly reach new levels of success and perfection. We (the people) have made in our society today a **perception** of *perfection* and that is **not** the reality of how life is. We live in a world of instant gratification in which has given many of us a non-realistic approach to life. So I've written this book, to inspire, encourage and to give some words of truth that we don't hear often enough.

When we are younger, we often think that opportunities are going to come our way fairly easily. However, that is not the case. As you grow up, you come to realize that life is not as easy as you thought it was going to be. It has many challenges, tests, trials and tribulations. You have to make many decisions; some easy, some difficult. It will impact the path of your journey. You must decide whether or not you will stay on the road to success. Success is not all about financial gains and titles, but about personal growth and development.

Why is it that the majority of the time circumstances have to be learned the hard way before it is learned at all? We must learn to be sensitive to our conscience and listen to our inner being. It is time to take responsibility for ourselves and our actions. I'm not only speaking to you, I'm also speaking to me. We all have faults and we all need some REAL TALK!

❝ What I am learning is that you cannot take on the world. All you can do is your best and let that be enough. ❞

—Miss Brit

Words hurt
Words heal
Words are very real.

Words hold power
Words hold truth
Words hold lies
Words are fruit.

>>> >>> >>> >>> >>>

On some real talk…

You are not confident with who you are and what you have to offer when you feel envious and threatened by someone else's gifts and talents.

Who society considers the most attractive people usually have the most problems with and within themselves. Remember that you are one of a kind. There is no comparison. We must do ourselves a favor and stop comparing ourselves to others. We must learn to appreciate and love ourselves for who we are.

Once you get over your insecurities, you will accomplish a lot more.

How we carry ourselves as individuals make all the difference of **how we are** and **who we are** collectively as a whole.

The way that you feel about yourself affects how others perceive you **and** how you treat other people.

It is hard to love when you don't love yourself or when you don't feel loved.

If you're always comparing yourself to others, you'll feel inadequate.

Don't let peer pressure or societies expectations become barriers in your mind.

What others say and think about you won't matter once you've realized your value and abilities.

The Glamorous Life
The illusion to your happiness

HOW TO FOREVER LOOK LIKE YOU'RE 21!

HOW TO LIVE LIKE THE RICH & FAMOUS

BEAUTY TIPS TO LOOK LIKE A STAR

HAVE YOUR OWN TEAM OF PAPARAZZI

0 23991 18471 9

Very often, the people with the most success and wealth forget about Who has blessed them with their riches and therefore it holds no value. Our wealth is worthless if it is all for the wrong reasons. It is very important to keep God in the forefront of your endeavors. Acknowledge God (Who is our main source) in everything. We must first have inner wealth before we can truly benefit from anything else.

When you eliminate God from your life, you automatically give the enemy the upper hand.

It doesn't matter what advantages you have on the outside if you are a mess on the inside.

Without God in your life, there's a piece of your inner self missing.

We the people are society. We make the world what it is by what we do, say and believe. Let's start doing the right things, saying the right words, and believing in the best regardless of whatever is going on around us. We must see opportunities in every situation. If we do our part, the trials will turn into triumphs.

It's time to start thinking the best and stop thinking the worst.

Speak positive affirmations over yourself. Your mind will eventually catch up.

If we are only focused on the bad, we'll miss out on the good. Seek the good.

Let's stop talking about changing for the better and **START** changing for the better.

Once you get the right motives in your heart, blessings will start to come your way.

God gives us all the free will of choice. In right choices, there are rewards and recompense. In wrong choices, there are lessons to be learned and consequences. Make the right decisions for yourself even when you don't feel like it or don't want to. It's for your benefit. Deep down inside, every person truly knows what the right choice is. Keep it real with yourself. Don't play yourself.

When you do the right thing and live the right way, someone always comes along to try to make you feel bad and get you off track. When that happens, continue to do right and live right anyway.

You want the breakthrough. However are you ready for the breakthrough?

When you feel like you're not going to get your breakthrough, you have to keep going because in reality, your blessing is right there in front of you.

Any challenge that you go through is right before the breakthrough.

You have to go through the rough times to get to the great times.

When you begin to wonder where your life is going, God takes you to the next level.

Too often, we get so wrapped up into other people's lives that we neglect our own.

We need to stop criticizing one another and take a good look at who we are. It is easy to talk about others while avoiding our own imperfections, yet it is hard to keep it real within ourselves about what needs to change in our own lives.

Give people room to be themselves. No one's perfect and neither are you!

We're each a work in progress. All you can do is your best.

When we worry about other people's lives, we miss out on our own.

Although the truth may hurt in the beginning, the truth heals in the end.

Why is it that we have selective hearing when it comes to hearing the truth? The truth helps us grow in character if we apply it.

Sometimes the things that are the hardest for us to hear are the things that we need to hear. It's in our best interest. It's called **TRUTH!**

What you don't want to believe is usually the inevitable truth.

The truth isn't always nice, yet the truth is always necessary.

We know the truth deep from within, yet we often ignore it.

The truth hurts our ego; however the truth gratifies the Spirit.

When <u>you</u> <u>are</u> <u>deceived</u> long enough, <u>deception</u> <u>becomes</u> **<u>your</u> <u>truth</u>**. Don't allow yourself to be deceived and don't deceive yourself.

At the end of it all (When it comes down to it), you **cannot** escape from the truth.

No matter how much you speak the truth, there will always be someone who doesn't want to listen.

Always stand for truth no matter what anyone else thinks. Truth is freedom.

The truth is at hand's reach. Grab it, hold onto it and don't ever let go!

TRUTH

INNER BEAUTY

PEACE VICTORY

HEALING JOY

FREEDOM

If we don't look at the bright side of life, we'll never enjoy it.

Invest in your future, live for today.

In the midst of working toward building your future, take the time to enjoy the present.

Live life!

Good intentions do not mean a thing if there's no action behind it.

You keep the promise not by making the promise, but **by living the promise**.

Your actions speak, talk is cheap!

You have to stay determined. You have to stay motivated. That is the only way you'll get to where you want to be. Each day you work toward your dream, the closer you become to living your dream.

Continue to consistently work at your God-given talent with diligence.

God + You= Dreams come true!

To reach each goal and to gain each achievement is a daily hustle and requires the ultimate drive, dedication, determination and motivation. The most important thing to remember about success is that it isn't the whole purpose of life, but just a small fraction of it.

Living your dreams is one of the most surreal experiences that you'll ever have.

You're telling a story with your everyday life. Make sure your story is good.

There are a lot of copies out there already, so be an original.

There's someone out there who is interested in what you have to say. Make sure it's worth hearing.

Learn to appreciate the simple things. It is often that the people <u>with the most</u> **appreciate it the least**. We must remember the true riches of life are the essence and blessings of everyday. Take gratitude in each day more and more.

Every day is a miracle because it's another day God created for us to enjoy!

Broaden your outlook on life.

We often see the potential of others, yet we don't see a great outlook for ourselves. We have to start being optimistic about our own future.

In the midst of reaching out to others, don't forget to reach out to yourself.

Don't underestimate your capability to reaching your highest potential.

K<u>nowing</u> <u>God</u> and the **<u>acknowledgement</u> <u>of</u> <u>God</u>** are two different things.

Knowledge is the intelligence of man. Wisdom is the intelligence of God. Knowledge without wisdom is **ignorance**.

Knowledge-Wisdom=Ignorance

Faith is putting confident action in what you believe God will do. God reacts to our action.

The points where your faith is being tested and strengthened in your life are the waiting periods: **Patience**.

Every difficulty that is encountered is a test of faith.

Ask yourself: Are my gifts and talents instilled in me worth taking a chance?

The closer your dreams come to a reality, the more afraid you may become and the tougher it may get. Work through your fears and the challenges along the way.

Anytime you take a chance, you don't know what the result is going to be.

No chance=No change

Prepare and build your dream to last.

It's not comfortable stepping outside of your comfort zone, however it is a necessary step toward your personal growth

The decision of one affects the lives of many.

You can't let the decisions of others stop you from living.

We often speak of they. Ask yourself, who are they? We are they!

Our thinking creates many of the results we see in our everyday lives through our words and actions.

Don't stress yourself out, regardless of the circumstances. Stress is a killjoy to your inner peace.

A mental calmness comes from with-in when you reach that place of letting go of worry and disappointments.

Until you let go of the pain, you haven't really forgiven.

Stop hiding your pain behind your smile. Let the tears fall. Do not internalize your pain. Crying is a healing process from it.

After you morn your pain, move forward and enjoy your life. Don't cry forever, so you can experience the delight!

When someone is continuously enabled, chances are that person will not become a responsible, productive citizen of society. Who are you enabling?

When you say you are not changing, what you are really saying is that you are **not** growing.

God gives us ALL courage from within. Each and every one of us needs to start using the courage within us to grow as people.

Real Talk Personal Point: *I'm sorry that you don't love me, but I have to love me. At times I wanted to be like everyone else. But then I realized that I can only be myself. How God created me is enough.*

The media and our society overall bombards us regularly with false ideals of beauty and success. You have to get yourself mentally to the place that you love, respect and appreciate yourself enough to know you are already equipped with everything that you need to succeed.

There will always be people and resources to try to make us give in and tear down our self-esteem. Therefore, learn **not** to be easily offended.

Even though you don't always win, you must **always maintain a winner's attitude**.

VICTORY

17

LYING! GO BACK TO THE THINKING ZONE

WATCH OUT! DISTRACTIONS FOLLOW YOUR HEART

13 **15**

12

you helped someone in need — YOU ARE BLESSED! MOVE FORWARD 6 SPACES

10

ALERT! made a mistake — SETBACK 3 SPACES

5 **THINKING ZONE — MAKING THINGS RIGHT** **7** **8**

made a true friend — MOVE FORWARD SPACE 10

3

GOOD LUCK

1

START

It takes more discipline of yourself to get more things done by yourself.

Sometimes you have to get away from the crowd to do what you need to do.

Fear not! For your blessings are at hand!

In the beginning it is scary getting out there on your own.

Fear is an illusion to keep you from progressing. Don't let fear, doubt or discouragement hinder your future.

Much fear is based upon how you may look in unfamiliar, complicated situations and what others will think about your response to it.

When you seize opportunities, even though you may be afraid or nervous, you often lead yourself into more opportunities and you learn more about yourself in the process.

Unrealistic expectations=Set up for failure

We often have a perception of life that is completely unrealistic; therefore we are setting ourselves up for disappointment when things don't turn out the way we expected.

When you try to fit in with society's standards, it will never be good enough, no matter how hard you try.

Two of the biggest challenges that God gives us is how to tolerate each other and to love one another.

Things are not always easy because people are not always easy going. Individually and collectively, we are very complex.

We need to have a welcoming attitude toward others.

We are often brought around unfriendly people because they are the ones who need kindness the most.

There are many people who we think don't deserve our kindness. We must still be willing to offer our kindness anyway. We have to show mercy not only to those who we know, but also on those who we do not know.

Everyone you try to reconnect with isn't going to remember you and some people don't want to remember you. That's just how it is. Move on!

We need to love one another. All we have is God and each other.

It's the imperfections of life that make it worthwhile. Be a student of life. Life is an ongoing lesson to be learned. You pay your dues throughout your everyday life.

Let your gifts and talents flow naturally. Greatness is not forced.

The smallest idea can turn into the largest investment.

Your talents and gifts will give you many opportunities, but only your maturity will keep you there. You must seek wisdom with diligence to sustain and maintain where your talents and gifts lead you.

Many of us are just concerned about obtaining a title (of accomplishment, rank or self importance), yet we often fail to accept the responsibility that it carries.

Don't always be the victim, instead be the survivor; be the over comer.

You have the power to turn your biggest tragedies into your biggest triumphs.

Staying upset is a waste of energy.

When you move on from bitterness, you move up in life.

$\mathcal{S}$ometimes what you think you want, you really **don't** want at all or <u>you</u> <u>are</u> **<u>not</u>** ready for.

Are you listening to God or are you listening to yourself?

There are times when we need to be quiet, listen, be sensitive to and follow God's guidance and let the plan reveal itself.

Everything is not always about you. Sometimes it is about others too. Let go of the ego!

You *hear* the message, but are you **listening** to the message? You *hear* me, but are you **listening**?

There is a point where you have to shut up and listen. Other people besides you have thoughts to share.

Case in point: *Know when to speak up, know when to shut up!*

You have to start somewhere. Otherwise you won't start at all.

Sometimes you have to start with hardly anything at all.

Start with where you're at. Work with what you have.

Make something of yourself whatever point you are at in your life. Make opportunities for yourself.

God can create something from little or nothing.

Home is always in your heart
Home humbles
Exploring the world expands
your outlook of all the possibilities
and opportunities available to you

GOD
FAMILY
FRIENDS
DREAMS
CAREER

The problem with so many of us today is that we try to keep up with the "Joneses". In other words, we try to keep up with what everyone else has. What we fail to realize is that people often put on a front and don't have as much as they say they have. Do not live beyond your means so that you can be more financially sound in the long run.

In order to receive more, you must first respect what you have.

FAME:
All That GLITTERS Isn't Gold

LONELINESS ARROGANCE
DECEPTION GREED
JEALOUSY ENVY
SELFISHNESS
TABLOIDS

A realization is the reality of what's really happening. A revelation is an inner understanding.

You don't have to keep telling someone when they're doing wrong because deep down inside, they already know.

You cannot help anyone who does not want to be helped. They first must decide to help themselves.

As difficult as it is, there comes a time where you have to stop worrying about what your family and friends are doing with their lives. They have to decide which path they are going to take. You cannot decide it for them.

We are often harder on the people closest to us than we are to the people who aren't. However, remember that we all grow and evolve at different times. Each person has to set a standard for themselves. We cannot set that standard for them.

Opportunity=Responsibility

We want more opportunities, yet we don't want the responsibilities that come along with it.

Sometimes you don't ask for more responsibility, it's just handed down to you.

When you face certain situations in life, it will force you to grow up.

A lot of people are not good parents because they are not ready to be nor have the desire to be a parent.

Being "friends with benefits" is a bad idea because feelings get involved no matter how hard you try to avoid it.

When you decide to have sex, you decide to potentially get pregnant or get someone pregnant.

For men who keep having babies with a variety of different women and women who keep having babies with a variety of different men: that is **NOT** a good look. It is time to put away the "assets"!

People allow sex to get them into unwanted situations by not exercising self discipline or responsibility.

"Freedom" is **not** an excuse to live a sloppy lifestyle.

Life-Boundaries=DESTRUCTION

𝓔verything will **not** always go according to your plans. Even though life doesn't always go the way you intended, you can always find something to be thankful for.

Don't let past disappointments stop you from being happy and enjoying each day.

You are <u>not</u> going to get closure in every situation. You should learn to let it be and move on.

You must diligently seek God to maintain balance and clarity in your life.

*C*ontrary to the people we read and hear about in the media, we still really don't know anything about them.

Just because you admire someone and what they do, doesn't mean you know them personally.

Just because a person is a so called "celebrity", it does not mean everything they do is right like the media often portrays.

It doesn't help to worry or complain because that doesn't make the situation change.

Certain situations in your life are not going to change until you've made up your mind that YOU are going to change.

Once you win the battles in your mind, you start to overcome and win the battles in your life.

You should inspire others but you should also have people in your life to inspire you.

When you are around constant negativity it takes a toll on your joy level.

The better quality of people that you are around, the better quality of life you'll have.

The company we keep is a crucial part of the harvest that we'll reap.

Learn to let go who and what isn't good for your life.

Unfortunately, everyone does not use their common sense.

Stop using nonsense and start using common sense.

Inform yourself. Ignorance is only bliss when you allow it to be.

Consistency is the key to getting results. If you're not consistent, don't expect good results.

The more you second guess yourself, the less you will progress.

You may not always produce your best work when you're committed to multiple tasks.

When you're involved in too many things, you do not have enough time to enjoy it.

Slow your roll. Don't be in such a rush to do everything. Take things one day at a time and receive the moment.

When you put less pressure on yourself, you can get more things accomplished. Focus only on the task at hand.

A woman who is truly loved and respected is a woman who carries herself with dignity and class.

A man who is truly loved and respected fully respects women and takes care of his responsibilities.

When a man gets jealous about a woman having her own success, chances are that man is insecure with himself and intimidated by her potential.

Ladies, do not hold a man back from raising and being a father to his children. Put your mixed emotions of a broken relationship aside. Your children **are not** leverage to get back at a man! It's about the child's well being. It's **ALL** about the child and **NOT** about you!

Don't lose yourself for someone else.

Another person does **not** define who you are. Yet complement one another with your own individuality.

Less is more. Simplify your life and your personal space.

Today's society motivates us to purchase things that we do not need. Get rid of and give away things on a regular basis. Less is more. You'll be amazed at how much better you would feel with a neat and tidy surrounding without clutter.

Less Clutter=More Balance

The quickest result is very often not the best result.

There is a high price for cheap thrills.

Your worldly gain is **NOT** worth your spiritual freedom. Spiritual freedom is priceless and worldly gain comes with a high cost.

Sometimes when you think the problem is with everyone else, the problem is really with **you**.

We often make excuses for ourselves when we know we are in the wrong. Take responsibility for your own actions!

Ask yourself, are you the creator of the conflict that surrounds you?

$\mathcal{E}$veryone does **not** have an easy going, laid back attitude and therefore are often difficult to communicate with.

Miscommunication often causes a lot of unnecessary problems and discord. Maintaining good communication is key.

Be confident in yourself and let your voice be heard. Build your confidence in order to communicate well with others.

When people take your kind nature for weakness, you have to demand your respect.

Everyone needs to hear **NO** sometimes.

You don't need to have your way all of the time.

There will be times when you are inconvenienced.

You are beautiful   *You are divine*

You are here, you are worth it

You are love

Trying to be someone else is a mask of the insecurities that lie within you. It is hard enough to be ourselves. There is no point in trying to be someone else. Learning to love yourself will help you accept and appreciate yourself for who you already are.

Regardless to what alterations we do to ourselves, at heart, we're still who we are since birth. The soul of our being does not change. Learn to appreciate your features and your gender. You are not a mistake. Own that truth!

We search for the beauty only to discover we had the beauty all along.

The essence of who we are is how God created us.

God is **not** going to help us be someone else.

You are not of your own.

Your physical imperfections are what make you unique. Learn to love you.

There will always be some one younger than you. There will always be someone older than you. Be content with the current stage you're at in your life.

Don't loathe yourself, love yourself.

What you want most is what you have to be the most patient for.

When you force things to happen they usually don't happen like they are suppose to.

Invest in your life now to receive the reward later.

With free will of choice comes great responsibility.

You can only live your life. Others can't live it for you. The decisions you make are completely up to you. Just always remember, you reap what you sow and the truth always finds you.

God is ultimately in control of our lives. However, we are in control of the way we live.

The choices you make: good or bad, can change your life in an instant.

We only have control over so much. There are certain things that are out of our hands, beyond our control. We need to respect and take responsibility of what we are in charge of and have control over.

Although in life things happen for a reason, much of it transpires in our lives due to **our choices**.

*D*on't sell yourself short in any relationship you encounter. If you want more for yourself, you must *require more of yourself* and then others will come to you with respect.

It's okay to be simply single!

It is important to take time to focus on you. Get yourself together!

Take the time to get your mind right and get your life right.

ESTABLISH YOURSELF FIRST!

When you take the time and responsibility to establish yourself first, you are building better opportunities to be more of a blessing to others and a better future for yourself.

Don't be ashamed to ask for help. It's okay. We all need help sometimes. But understand that you must eventually learn to sustain consistently on your own.

You have to make your own life for yourself. No one else can make it for you.

You have to take care of yourself before you can help anyone else.

There are many paths to following and living your dreams. However, your path may not be the path of someone else's. Let God lead you into the path of success. Step out in faith.

Stop holding yourself back and letting others hold you back from fulfilling and living your dreams.

The time to work on your dreams is now! Besides, you have nothing else better to do if you think about it. God didn't give us gifts and talents for nothing. Use them in a positive way to make the world a little bit better and a little bit brighter.

Don't allow others to allow you to miss the simplicity of God.

God leads you to potential and great opportunities when you aren't even looking for them.

There are no friends when it comes down to business and money.

Know your business. Do not be ignorant with your financial standing. Learn to budget your income and become responsible with ALL of your resources.

No money is free money. Something is always required in return.

It's not always about making money. It's about keeping your sanity.

Money: Save, Give, and spend some. Do **not** spend all the money you have! Create a budget that will help you utilize all of your finances.

Ignoring the problem is not going to solve it. You must confront the adversity.

If you created the problem, provide a fair solution. If you didn't create the problem, it doesn't help to gripe about it.

You must decide to be happy. Others cannot maintain your level of happiness.

If you wait to be happy, you won't be happy.

Don't be a prisoner of circumstances.

Holding on to sadness and negativity will keep you in bondage.

When you do not see a reason to be happy, be happy for no reason and you will find that the answer lies within your state of mind.

There is no avoiding hardship. Everyone encounters it. You have to have hard times in order to go to the next level.

Our lives get shaken up every once in a while. It's how we handle the shake ups that count.

It's easy to say that you'll be faithful when you're not going through the hardships of life. The hardships are the test that strengthens your faith and character.

Have a compassionate attitude toward others going through tough ordeals because it could be you.

The hardest times of your life are often the most humbling times. The hard times humble you for the good times.

During questionable and unstable times, the basic, regular routines and daily small blessings we often take for granted, begin to take on more meaning.

Times of uncertainty are times to trust God more than ever.

Don't forget about God in the midst of your victories and prosperity. We must continue to have a humble and grateful attitude toward God and others in the good times.

Gratitude is a way of contentment.

All the prosperity you gain is in vain if you do not give credit to the source from which it came.

More isn't always necessarily better. Make sure you appreciate the place you're at in your life before you go after more.

When you spend less, you waste less.

When you continue to squander what you have, nothing will ever seem to suffice.

Make peace, not drama.

If you speak peace, you get peace.

When there is no love in the home, there is no peace in the home.

We have the tendency to overrate things and make a bigger deal out of it than it really is.

Don't fall for the media or societies scare tactics. They often mislead the public and put people in an unnecessary panic and fear mode.

Keep the faith in every situation despite all of the daily speculation.

Fear paralyzes your progress. What have you allowed fear to stop you from doing?

You cannot spend your life being afraid. Otherwise you are not really living, you just exist.

Start off as a sideliner to eventually become a headliner!

Just because you're in a bad environment doesn't mean that you have to become a product of it. Aspire to go beyond your bad surroundings.

Don't count yourself out for extraordinary opportunities.

Many small steps lead into the huge step of success!

Don't sell out or put out to gain notoriety and opportunity. Don't compromise your core morals and values for society's standards.

Decisions based on greed, stereotypes, prejudice, hate and selfishness have created the unjust and unfair conditions and circumstances in our society.

It's the crooked and conniving ways of people in certain situations that halt the extended progress that we could be making. There are no long term benefits in being a part of a con. The truth always prevails at any given time. You will get caught!

Networking is the key to advancement. A lot of times what determines the job you get are the people that you know.

Just because someone impresses you with their personality and credentials at a job interview doesn't mean they're going to be a productive worker.

Many times when other people don't do their job correctly, everyone else usually ends up having to deal with the consequences of it.

Poor work ethic leads to poor leadership.

Many of us live a lie so we don't have to face the truth. However in the end, the reality is that we've cheated ourselves and others from knowing who we really are.

It takes a lot of courage to be honest with yourself.

We all have our quirky and awkward moments. It's a part of personal growth.

Everyone has the capability to look presentable. Your appearance contributes to your success. Dress to succeed. If you do not take yourself seriously no one else will either. Come correct or don't come at all!

Keeping your appearance and hygiene together share equal priority.

Each and every person has something worthwhile to contribute.

The enemy constantly puts thoughts in our minds to make us feel that we're inadequate of doing the things we want in life. We must remember that we <u>are</u> <u>capable</u> because **GOD** made us **ALL** capable.

Each and every day is a new opportunity to do something great and to be someone great. That someone is you!

It's easier to encourage and motivate others. It is the hardest to encourage yourself.

It's not enough for others to cheer you on. You have to cheer yourself on to build up your confidence.

Don't discourage---**ENCOURAGE**.

It's easy to be happy for those you get along with. It's hard to be happy for those you can't stand.

Often the people and things that annoy us most, we end up missing the most when we no longer have them. Cherish who and what you have every day.

The "good life" doesn't come easy. If often comes with a price.

Many times we get so caught up in the glamour of things that we forget about the reality.

The more you have the more you're going to deal with.

We often want to acquire more things for our own selfish motives.

Many of us become envious of the glamorous lifestyle due to the fact that we are not living it. However, it's not easy to get to that place and it is not all that it seems.

As far as fame and recognition goes, a lot of us want the attention for the wrongs reasons or no reason at all. That's why we don't receive it. Furthermore the platform that involves fame isn't for everybody.

You think that you're missing out on something because you're not doing what everyone else is doing. The truth of the matter is that you're **not** missing out on anything at all.

Many people will put on a front (*self-importance*) of how they want their lives to be perceived by others.

Putting on a front is false validation.

If you've got it, you don't have to brag about it. People who feel the need to constantly brag about their possessions, usually aren't doing as well as they make it seem.

Many people are not mentally ready or mature enough to get married. For this reason, many marriages do not last.

Do **NOT** get married for the wrong reasons!

Before even considering marriage, make sure that you are friends first.

Marriage is a work in progress that requires embracing the whole person. Do not except the engagement if you are not willing to be patient and dedicated to one person. Just because you <u>think</u> you're ready to get married doesn't mean that you are. Once you say "I do" it is no longer all about you.

Only marry a person if you LOVE them. Any other reason is invalid.

Love is expressed through your daily actions.

People fall in love with the idea of falling "in love" and come to find out that they were never in love at all.

It is those who we usually want to love us most that usually don't love us at all.

Love has no color, yet are you loving or lusting after someone because of their color?

Society has a false identity of love. Love is not vain or superficial.

Real love is not built on betrayal or deceit.

Love or Lust?
Is this engagement for you?

Just as you cannot make anyone change, you cannot make anyone love you.

Loving someone and *being in love* with someone are two entirely different concepts.

It is a waste of time to be involved in a relationship with someone whom you have no interest.

Don't make life altering decisions by impulse or emotions. Feelings change.

It is unwise to live your life completely based on your feelings and emotions alone because it leads to making unwise decisions.

We may not be able to control certain thoughts and feelings that come over us at times, however it is **OUR CHOICE** whether or not we act upon those thoughts and feelings. Will you choose to redirect your thoughts?

Prejudice and greed holds us back as a society. ENOUGH ALREADY!

In order to have better relationships, we must be willing to become better people.

When we communicate with each other, we help one another grow into better individuals. When we grow individually, we start growing as a society.

The human race as a whole: Together we are powerful, apart we are powerless.

Sometimes you have to go through certain experiences on your own to have a change of heart later on. Just make sure that you're not too late.

God loves us so much that sometimes He has to save us from ourselves.

Some people don't change the negative aspects in their lives until they're on the edge of destruction. Are you living on the edge?

Bad moods and attitudes: We all have our moments. However we have to learn to keep it in check and know when to let the negative feelings and emotions go.

A lot of times the petty and spiteful attitudes and feelings we have toward others lies deep within. Learn to slowly let go of those feelings by having a kind nature on purpose and eventually those feelings and attitudes within you will start to slowly subside.

There will always be someone to hate on you. Get used to it and move on. The only reason you're getting hated on is because the other person is insecure. Or they may see something in you that they like or want something or someone that you have in your life. Don't let it phase you. Don't waste your time listening to nonsense. Ask yourself are you the insecure one? Be honest with yourself!

Jealously and envy are very unattractive. Wear the attitude of humility instead.

Don't covet (don't be envious or jealous of) who or what anyone else has. God has created unique blessings designed just for you!

You can**not** buy respect! Money **won't** buy you respect. It's the true sincerity of your character and personality that earns you respect from others.

Work is your livelihood for your financial means, but it is not your life.

Technology has connected us, yet disconnected us from one another. Personal interaction is lacking.

We must make time for ourselves, our family and friends.

Giving to others is a way to humble self.

It's not about how much you give, but whether you're giving from your heart. Ask yourself, is your generosity genuine?

Love is sincere acts of kindness.

It is important that we love God simply for who He is and not only for what He can and is able to do for us. Love God because He is God.

Honor God with your everyday life. Honor God with your mind, mouth, attitude and actions.

In unexplainable times, don't run away from God, run toward Him.

You choose what you do and don't do. The choice is yours.

You cannot do everything, but you can do something. Make a difference.

Why is it that we start caring when it is too late to care? Why didn't we care all along?

Do not wait for desperate times to occur before unity happens. UNITE NOW! UNITY NOW!

𝒯imes of hardship should be times of reevaluating.

Some of the hardest things that we go through are the things that have the most significance and prepare us for new levels in life.

All the challenges you go through is God's way of preparing you for something better.

God's plan is always better than the plan that we have for ourselves.

People often have a lot on their minds and on their hearts that they never speak about. Keep it real with yourself first and foremost and with others. However, we have to choose our words carefully and be tactful with what we say. In all honesty, sometimes, the truth hurts and everyone is not going to like it.

If you have something to say to someone, it is just best to say it! People often want to tell you something and never get around to it. Speak up! I can't hear you!

Whether you realize it or not, you're making an impact on someone's life.

The image you portray is how others will view you.

When you get too comfortable, you get lazy and become complacent. In retrospective, it makes it harder for you to adjust to change.

When you become lazy, you have to become active on purpose.

When your mind is not occupied with something positive to do, careless choices and decisions are often made. It is vital that you don't keep your mind idle.

Don't waste time with procrastination or any conversation or situation that is not adding value to your life.

Time is valuable. Time is moving. Don't waste it!

Assumptions and misunderstandings bring unnecessary tension and conflict.

Never assume the assumption because you might be wrong.

Get to know a person first. Your initial perception may be wrong. Sometimes the assumptions you make are the complete opposite of the reality. Seek out the good qualities in people and follow your intuition. Find out the facts first.

Don't listen to hearsay; evaluate the situation or individual for yourself.

We get too wrapped up into each other's assumptions, negative opinions and hearsay. Let's speak better of one another.

If you start to focus more on what you're doing right, what you're doing wrong will start to change.

If you balance your mindset, your life will become balanced.

Build up your thoughts, build up your life.

If you think victorious, you live victorious.

If you build your patience, you build your faith.

True Love
Where does thy heart lie?

FRIENDSHIP

COMMITMENT

BETRAYAL

HONESTY

HYPOCRISY

EGO

COMPANY

You never know what your act of kindness may mean to another person.

When you're kind to others, that kindness may or may not be reciprocated back to you. Continue to be kind anyway.

Love a person for who they are, not only for what they can do for you. That is appreciated far more beyond words.

Be considerate to everyone. You never know who you'll meet or how they could change your life.

The smallest, simplest acts of kindness can make a huge difference.

𝒫ray. Stay grateful. Stay faithful.

Pray about **EVERYTHING**. Even the stuff you may think or feel are insignificant, pray about it anyway.

There is a fine line between confidence and cockiness.

Arrogance is **NOT** attractive.

When you start getting to know God, you start getting over yourself.

*R*eal Talk...

Building a better you...

Building a better life...

Building a better world...

One day at a time.

When you love and respect yourself and others and when you have peace in your heart that is the definition of *true success*.

It's the greatness of living up to or beyond our potential that scares us the most.

Do not be afraid of the greatness that God has placed in YOU!

We all have weaknesses that we need to overcome.

We have all done things that we are not proud of, however it is never too late to start over.

Daily Real Talk:
Communication and Conversations with One Another

1. Turn off **ALL** electronics and cell phones before preceding any conversations listed below.

2. Have a sit down dinner discussion at least three times a week.

3. Have regular designated times for sit down discussions with family and friends.

4. Be open to listen to each other's views and feelings of one another positive and negative.

5. Have open debates in your community about a variety of topics and issues.

6. *Be completely honest with one another in the conversations that you have.

7. *Watch how you communicate when you are mad, irritated or disappointed about something because it could come off in the wrong way or a more negative way than you intended.

*Remember: Better communication with one another will eventually lead to more honest and better relationships over time.

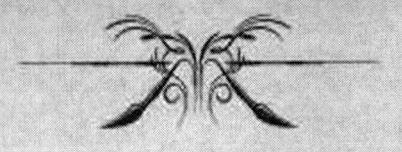

Designed by
Luciana Luraschi

Designer
Illustrator
Drawer

Portfolio at

www.lucianaluraschi.jimdo.com

Contact

luci.luraschi.93@hotmail.com

Gem Star

For booking information,
general inquiries or
to send your feedback,
please contact Miss Brit at:

gemstarmedia1@yahoo.com